DEAR YA ROUHI

HOW MY LIFE CHANGED AFTER HER FRIEND REQUEST

KAVIN

pencil

ISBN 978-93-5610-761-8
© KAVIN 2022
Published in India 2022 by Pencil

Contributors:
Co-Author: Iswarya
Co-Author: Iswarya

A brand of
One Point Six Technologies Pvt. Ltd.
123, Building J2, Shram Seva Premises,
Wadala Truck Terminal, Wadala (E)
Mumbai 400037, Maharashtra, INDIA
E connect@thepencilapp.com
W www.thepencilapp.com

Author biography

Hey this is kavin ,from chennai..I am not an author and all , i just wrote our real fairy tale to make my girl's birthday more special...

CONTENTS

YA ROUHI

Path to destiny.

"Every love story is beautiful B ut ours is my favourite"

(To my special person)

Before getting into my path to destiny, **HAPPY BIRTHDAY ISWARYA ITS JUNE 5TH 2022 ,** I was soo confused about how to make your birthday even more special, i didn't got any idea or even i couldn't able to gift you anything because of this distance ..Hope this make your birthday special once again **HAPPY BIRTHDAY MY BETTER HALF...Love you always and forever**

HOW I WAS BEEN BEFORE HER:(

When I was in 11th grade, I wasn't interested in love, and that was because I had a bad past, it's not a bad past, it's actually the worst ..On that point i used to be simply flirting with a few random girls due to the fact i used to be now no longer inquisitive about love..few girls used to flirt with me and few proposed me..

FROM (24-5-2018)

Lets get into the story ,path to destiny ,my life changing moment,door to happiness etc ...I got my first cell phone on may 24th .. but I had no one to talk . however I had nobody to speak It's simply to play games, and my friends made me download Instagram but i didn't know any heck about it..

HOW I MET MY ROUHI (29-9-2018)

It was just a typical day until September 29, 2018.Here begins my life's fairy tale.I still remember it was Saturday night around 10 pm ...I obtained a request on Instagram from a person I do not know..Her Instagram name was iswarya something i dont remember ..I accepted her request and she has five or six photos in her account.. I flattered as quickly as I noticed her....

She was such a pretty girl..On that night time we talked for a while and she went to sleep..I started flirting with her without a second thought.. I don't know who she was, where she was, is she committed or not literally I don't know anything about her..It's my gut that makes me think she's my girlfriend..Sunday I had a cricket match before I went over there, we had a little conversation.. Like flirty conversation And I went to the game, but I didn't had an awesome game..I came back home with a smile because she was waiting for me..I thought about asking her if she is interested in love, but I have no idea about her..After some time i planned to propose her but i had no idea how to propose her ,i know to propose girls but she is not just a girl she is more than that like an angel ..at the same time i wish to propose her differently because i dont want to propose her simply like everyone do..I tried to trick her so I told her that i like a girl but dont know how to propose , and asked her that can i practice here and told her to correct me if it is not okay.. i I proposed her, then she said yeah it was good and told me to go ahead..After some time ishu asked me whether i proposed the girl i like or not. and i told yeah i proposed and she told like, it was good and told me to go ahead..Ishu was confused for a bit..But after a while she asked me heyyy did you proposed me for real ?? And i simply told yeah I love you iswarya i dont know who you are and where you are i dont care about it ..

"The greatest love story is when you fall in love with the unexpected person at the most unexpected time"

Till now i dont know why i proposed her ..I just felt like she is the one for me..Then she asked me whether i will be true or not , then she asked me to promise her that i will never leave..That time ,We both dont know what love is but still we managed somehow..She was soo cute ..she was in 10th grade that time...and she used to braid her hair ..she would look like more traditional then, but now vice versa ..

now she's more into fashion..That traditional ishu has become more modern girl..I like both she looks pretty in both traditional and modern..Lets get back to the story, after some strict rules she accepted my love i mean our puppy love..Then we started talking a lot after schl timee we started texting a lot..We haven't had phone calls that much.. SHE IS MORE INTELLIGENT, SHE IS A TOPPER,she used to study alot ..we cant speak during weekdays because she wont use her phone in weekdays ..She has followed strict rules and thats because her mom is maths teacher.. So we used talk more.on weekends..

Then October 2nd i posted a video song on Instagram for her...That song was about her like, iswarya are you ready huh ,veeta vitu enkuda than neeyum variya (are you ready to come with me ,out of your house) ..I posted this song for her ..But unfortunately that time i didn't know☐it would be cringy but fine it was cute moments for us...I used to do tik tok videos that time ,she liked it very much ..she suggested a audio and asked me to do a video of that song..And i did that video on that day itself.. (love tickets la lottery adichachu ,dark uh night uh empty streeet uh mutham onnu tharuvaya) this is the song she suggested me ..

Then one day some random guy commented badly on her post and i fought with him ,we were scolding each other ,and the next day ishu came to know what happened ..She cried on her school because she was so sensitive and more like baby .And she fought with him scolded him badly for me.. We will never forget those moments..After everything, We were talking comfortably, we became close..But we haven't talked romantic and all because we don't know anything about it we were just like more than a friend ..I liked her so much but i dont know why, it all happened just like that..I still believe she has been sent to me by god.I dont know how she found my account in her suggestions but that single request from her it changed our whole life..She is from Coimbatore and i am from chennai..She used to study all the time, so we don't talk often..I showed my friends a picture of her and they were jealous of me..She looks like a Brahmin girl even i asked her that are u vegan but she is not ..

We promised each other not to leave at any situation..It was all good until November because i started thinking whether i am doing right or not, started to question myself if this relationship would work or not..But i am sure i liked her so much..I was soo confused that time and i started avoiding her ,but i regret now..I stopped replying her texts,i stopped talking with her ..She started texting my friends to contact me..It was the worst part of our life..She is a very good girl i shouldn't have done like that to her ,she doesn't deserve that ..She was soo sweet girl.. I had no idea how to discuss about how i felt..Then i lied to her that my mom saw everything and scolded not to talk with her..Then she said nothing but i know she was soo sad ..I regret alot..We Stopped talking, thats it all over... I missed her because of my stupid mind..

After 3 months , I made my mind clear..I wanted to talk with her again..I searched her in Instagram but i didn't got her account..I asked her friend about iswarya and they told that she got cought by her mother while using Instagram and told her to delete Instagram..I knew her number but i didn't call her because i dont want her to get into trouble..I couldn't able to contact her even her friends Never helped me..I used to tell her every friends to tell ishwarya that i asked her ..I am the who avoided her , i shouldn't have done like that ..And i deserved sufferings..I missed her so much..But i never stopped asking her friends about her..

After that we didn't talked for months literally..I thought everything was over ..But one day i got a chance to contact her i think its 2019 i dont remember which month..I talked with her and asked how she was doing etc...I apologized to her.. Actually she was in some birthday party , she told to call but i was in home with my sister soo i couldn't..After some time i lied to my mom that i am going to study with my friend in his home...But i didn't went to his home actually i took my cycle and went inside the park to talk with her .. Because i dont want to loose this chance ..I called her and we talked for some time...I asked her why didn't u wished me on my birthday ,she just smiled..Then i came home ..Then she again called me at around 7 30 ..We talked for 5 minutes ,its just normal casual talk..I asked if you'd talk to me every day , she said maybe ..

Then we started talking daily , i mean just normal casual talk.. it is all what i wanted that time ..Even i proposed her again but she is not ready to trust me again..But we talked only for one month.. All of a sudden she blocked me without saying anything ..I asked about ishu to her friends but didn't got a proper reply..Then i itself understood that she has moved on already..Back to normal mode without her text .. Without iswarya voice ..But i couldn't move on..I was so low and i badly wanted her..She was far away from me ..I asked her friends to add conference but she didn't picked up because she was afraid of me ..One day while i am going to ground i called her number and she took the phone and i said ishwarya are u there but She got off the phone when she heard my voice..It was her father's number, actually, but I was hoping she'd come on the phone..After that she blocked me in Normal call too..

I got a phone call from her friend and she told not to call ishu..I asked her friend to add ishu to call ..Then after 2 minutes ishu came and i asked her what happened ishwarya why did u blocked me ..she said nothing she was silent for a minute then i told lets not talk if u don't want to talk with me then she hung up the phone.And I was ok with it..And i got a text from her friend that ishu was getting ready for her neet class and also she told not to text ishu..After that i Never tried to contact ishu..I ill just ask her friends how ishu was doing..

Suddenly after months i felt soo low and wanted to talk with her ..I was thinking about how to contact her. its actually 2019 Ganesh chaturthi day i think..I lied to her as I cut my hands with a blade.. and i sent some photos which i actually Googled..She got spooked and called me immediately..I was like so happy thst she called me and i acted like a fool..She asked me why and how ..i acted like i was crying and she told me to tell my mom about my hand ..She cared me soo much..but i didn't felt guilty because she was talking with me thats what i wanted exactly soo i continued..I asked her will u love me or not ,and she said yes i do..Even that day also she was getting ready for some function soo she went after that..

But she didn't loved me at all, she just said yes to make me smile..After a day her friends told that she was interested on someone and that boy stopped talking with her so she was in depression...I asked her about that she was not ready to talk about that ..Then i felt sad for her and stopped disturbing her because i dont want to pressure her anymore..I never stopped loving her even though she is not interested on me..I waited for her. I came to know that she was not okay ..I dont want to say his name who just time passed her by talking ..As i already told she was soo sensitive she cant handle anything..She ill cry for small small things .. Her friends told that she was taking councellings..I felt really bad.. After that i stopped thinking and contacting her..But i never stopped asking about ishu to her friends..I left her only oncee after that i never stopped loving her..I decided not to love anyone else because i literally dont want anyone in her place..Soo i started waiting for her ,i wanted to make her happy, and i dont wanted her to be cheated by someone else again soo i waited for her ..And i was ready to accept her even after knowing everything because getting a true person in life is all every boys wants , That too in this fake world..For me she was always correct ,i never saw a girl like her.. Loyalty=iswarya for me..

I stopped thinking about her because 12th exams dates were close...So i started preparing for my examss.. That was the time, covid started spreading slightly in india..And the TN government announced full lockdown from 24th march 2020 after my last exam ...

HOWCOVIDHELPEDUSTO GET INTOLOVEAGAI N(but not like before, for permanent):

" HERE STARTS OUR FAIRY TALE KAVIN ISWARYA"

Here we go.. After my last board exam they announced full lockdown..So i started sleeping late at nights and waking up at afternoon..I watched a bunch of movies...I watched whole Avengers series..I just watched movies all the time ..I started working out..Had soo much fun in the lockdown..I completely forgot ishuu...

It was just a regular day till the evening

of April 10..Was watching some sai pallavi s Hindi movie, because she resembles iswaryaa...Was thinking about iswarya while watching movie.. I was just scrolling whatsapp contacts ..I had all the numbers of ishu..Then i saw a profile of her..But i was not sure whether its her or her mom.. I continued watching the movie thinking of her..

And the day has arrived ITS APRIL 11TH 2020.. I texted her hii..She blocked me☐ however i was aware of it already that she could block me.. Then, in a minute, I got a message from her friend.. She told not to text ishuu..And here lied her once more that i got covid...and told her friend to inform iswarya.. Then i got a call from her friend she brought Iswarya too..I still have the call records, we talked that day...She was asking about my health..and i was lying to her...We talked after soo many months..She hesitated to talk however it was cute☐..And i was also asking about her health..And i told her that i still love you and waiting for you...she simply smiled.... told her to text me in Instagram ..I asked her whose number is this and she said it was my mother's number but i already know that it was her number. Her mother called her and she stopped by, said I'll text you later..I was waiting for her text but i didn't got any text from her, that day..But after a day, eventually i got a text from her..She asked about my fever, but I wasn't ill at all..I said I was better after seeing your message. She laughed, that is what I needed..We texted for some time..She said she was going to block me because her mom may check her phone.. Then she blocked me and informed Will text you tomorrow..She become little bit scared to have a conversation..

Then she started texting with me... I would be waiting for her always because she wont be coming online often..I've even muted everyone except her because I do not need to get disappointed thinking it was her.. I Used to wait in her page to come online she would come however not to my page which hurts..thats because we started fresh,this time its now no longer like before,she even hesitated to talk..She attempted to keep away from me because she wanted me to move without thinking about her always, but She never said a thing about it that time, she said it only after we got commited..

And right here after a few ordinary days,I started flirting her as if this is the first time i'm talking with her, its all fate..I even used to get up early morning to reply her text however she wont be there while i respond, then i would sleep again..I even changed the sound of her notification for two main reason, one is to be always available for her, no matter whether or not its day or night time.. second is she wont come to WhatsApp regularly so i dont need to miss the chance to text with her..Then she started replying me quicker than before and that i impressed her Little bit by waking up earlier to reply her text.. Somehow she started calling me..We used to talk for few minutes that too she wont talk anything, she could simply respond however it turned into adorable though..

We both started talking comfortably she also felt comfortable with me, on the begin she dont even respond to my text however now contrary of it,she started calling me..I still have those call records of us, sweet conversation of us..That is the time i started work outs,the only good habit i had however once we started talking all of it went off jus like that..She could say maybe maybe for everything i asked..I actually started hating that phrase due to her..Our phone call period started increasing from 20 minutes to hours..I showed her how much i really like her and the way i waited for her..We shared many stuff actually we had been like buddies again,however she know my intention ...I by no means compelled her to like me ..I even adviced her like a well wisher.. And one day, was texting her continuosly and she said "have some patients baby"...Thats the primary time she is calling me baby after soo long time...I even requested her to call me baby one extra time so that i can take screenshot..I still have many screenshots of our text we exchanged

June 5 is her birthday..I wished her in advance before 15 days itself.. My wish was the first wish for her and nevertheless i'm the one who wishes her first..Its june 4th night,was waiting for 12 am to wish her...I typed lengthy paragraphs to wish her ,wished her finally..She said, my wish was the bestest in her life and i was super glad to hear that ...Was expecting her to come because soo many people had been wishing her..She told me to sleep but i said its fine i will wait for u and lets both go to sleep at the same time and she was okay with it...Then we each went to sleep after saying goodnights and all kind of things.. Next day morning she was wearing mild yellow or green maxi with out sleeves..She shared a few photos, i still have all those photos...She also sent one video of her getting surprised by her friend madhu, gifted her a photo frame, thats the first time i was listening to her voice louder ..In that video she said, OMG itha nan expect eh panalanuuu, she became shouting literally..But unfortunately we could not able speak on phone call because she blocked me once more with out saying anything but i was expecting her call however she didn't...

I thought she vanished once more like she usually do but she did not she unblocked me after 1 day..I asked her why and she said that she was sad and not in the talking terms ..I let her to take her time to feel comfortable.. My path to destiny continued, We become more closer than ever and shared each little issue happened in past..We used have fun through sharing our past stories, we actually shared the whole thing with out hiding anything.. The day has come its "twenty fourth june 2020" she finally accepted me..I gave her time, let her to feel comfortable ,i by no means pressured to like me,..24th June morning she said like i love u but shall we hold like this till i complete my 10th grade,I become absolutely okay with her and i said yeahh thats great i will wait for u and i've been waiting for her soo long so its now no longer a big deal to wait one extra year.. The twist was,after a while she said love u and i was like confused for a second and asked her, after 10th only righttt then she said no ..She said she's ready to accept me .. This is how our tragedic love tale changed into faity tale..After plenty and plenty of confusion,breaks, we become strong in our relationship ..Later that day,we had a cringy conversation , that time we didn't realize that we're doing cringe however now every time we think about it we used laugh like anything..

Our love bloomed again,however this time its definitely special from before, we knew what love is and we knew the way it all work.. This time i felt love is more important than the distance we had.. "Distance doesnt be counted while people trust each other".. So many boys proposed her and a few girls proposed me however God had a few different plan for us.. We in no way thought we'd get committed, we still believe this love its all because of god ..Our love tale was written by the hand of God ...

DEAR GOD I WANT TO THANKYOU FOR MY BEAUTIFUL PARTNER..THE ONE SINGLE REQUEST FROM HER ,IT CHANGED OUR WHOLE LIFE .. WILL NEVER EVER FORGET HOW I GOT HER AND WILL NEVER LEAVE HER OR TREAT HER BAD ..

Then later the day,in the night we had been talking about how much we both love each other.. We had been arguing about who's extra fortunate in our relationship..I trusted her blindly due to the fact i knew she was the one who can be my partner.. Rajesh ,he's the one with whom i will share everything he was the first person to know about our relationship.. Then ishu and me had a overwhelming conversations,its like my dream come true moment because that point i did not had some other Dreams rather than her .. To be frank until now i dont have any dreams..My only dream is to be happy with her and she becoming doctor..Her achievement is my achievement,her happiness is my happiness. i know, it could be cringy to listen this however thats the fact..

After that my every day workouts changed ..ishu and me started talking for two to three hours due to the fact her mother will not be in home due to her school works, she is a teacher that too maths teacher i hate maths...So one day nighttime she wore a saree she desired me to look her i told her to take pics but she did a video call, That is our first video call..I turned into little bit anxious even she too,i informed her that i'm with out a shirt but she said its fine we could make vc.. Then i called her, even this is the first time i'm seeing her in saree..She looked sooo cute like a doll, i recorded that entire video call i still have those..She was literally like a stick in that saree but cute though..

Nothing exciting after that we simply used to speak for more than four hours constantly however we had nothing to talk about we each could be pronouncing then then then for hours.. Obviously a few cringy matters too.. Wil never overlook how i were given her...We become soo close we both never imagined a existence like we're together its all that request..If i will keep a name for our existence or our relationship that could be "request from an angel"..After she got here into my life in 2019 i never desired a woman other than her, just like that everything changed she turn out to be mine i never anticipated though..She has constantly been there for me in each situation happy or sad,good or terrible its constantly her who been there for me..I knew i wont get any real soul than her.. Nowadays it is too difficult to find a lover that too genuine girl like her its not possible however i'm blessed to have her my side...

Then we had our first fight i dont remember the date correctly however one night time i shouted her like silly after which next day i avoided her ..Her friend sent me an screenshot of her text in that text she was like i miss him,i need to speak with him and sort of things had been there after i noticed that my heart melted ..Then what, we had been cuddling via texts no other go this fucking distance..Its August 16th night time round 11 30 the following day was my birthday..For the first time i called her wifey then she was like greatly surprised for a second she was blushing i knew that via her text itself..Then she was the first person to wish me..She wrote a few paragraph which means alot for me.. Because nobody wished me the way she did.. So obviously it turned into special to get a wish from special person.. Till now she is my best friend I am Really truly blessed to find both a love and friendship in the same person

FIRSTEVERMEET (19-1-2021)

Then after a few weeks we started fighting like tom and jerry..we both used to be scolding each other badly....After a few months we started planning to meet..we had been jus making plans to meet ..We deliberate to meet at January month.. due to the fact that point i had my sister's marriage at January 17..Soo i was there in Madurai..That is the time corona cases started reducing and that they had been making plans to begin schools and colleges..Her mother started going to school..Soo we planned to meet at her home..I informed my dad and mom that i will go to my friend home for two days stay...they said ok to it.. Then i booked bus from madurai to Coimbatore..I became soo worried due to the fact i've never travelled by myself or went some other city with out my dad and mom ..she was nervous too because this is the first time we going to meet ..My friends had been there with me,they came to my sister's marriage.. January 18th i dropped my friends at railway station they had been going chennai back..Soo after i dropped them i was actually awaiting 2 hours 30 minutes for my bus.. Was listening our favourite music continuously.. My bus was at 11 45..we end up so nervous ..My bus came.. Finnally i reached coimbatore round five 30 am... did not booked any inn that point soo planned to wait till mrng 9 30 for her mom and dad to leave home....So was simply listening to musics and roaming right here and there.. We both were soo happy that we're in the same city .. That is the first time traveling coimbatore..I became very excited to meet her.. however at one aspect we had been Nervous too...

I had my breakfast at arvis hotel opposite to gandhipuram bus stop..after which i changed my dress there..After completing my breakfast..was seeking out a few bouquet shop and i found one.. It was round 1km ..I by no means in my life walked for a km i did not realize that it might be too long to walk..I walked with the assist of map and i found that shop.. bought bouquet for her.. First time in my life buying flowers for a girl..Soo i booked ola from there to gandhipuram once more because i knew now that i can not walk that much distance..It was round eight o clock i bought a few chocolates,cakes, ice cream, kinder joy she likes it very a lot until now,etc... After that was waiting in that backery..After her mom and dad leaves she called me and informed to book ola to kovilmedu bus stop..She was in call we were talking ..I was telling that right here i'm now and told our distance is started decreasing..I reached close to her school from her school it is just 1 km to her home..We both become nervous..I reached bus stop got off from the car and she told me walk in straight....She asked me can u see the appartments and i was like i told yeahh there is some round round appartment ..She asked me can u see the appartments and I told yeahh there's a few round round appartment...

Actually i named that appartment as round round appartment, until now we used to address it like that manner only..So she informed me to walk straight,

She saw me and i saw her however her face was not clear because she was in her house first floor .. she came down and bumped into her house after seeing me the instant we noticed, i still remember.. We were still on the phone call she informed me to open the door and move inside the first floor house.. No one was there because they constructed that only before few months..Soo became anticipating her to come ..We had been actually talking very well untill we ended up the call ..She came inside the room and that i gave her a proper hug and gave the bouquet to her she was shocked..Gave all of the chocolates ,she asked why this much and i was like it is fine have it...I requested her a charger she became soo nervous even i too.. Literally we were talking with out seeing each other eyes we both were so nervous...she went right all the way down to bring me a charger.. Was anticipating her to come..she came and i hugged her, A warm hug. We had been hugging for a while and patting each other's shoulders.. We could never forget our first tight hugss...The second we had been yearning for..we were like yeahh its Finally happening..we made it .it has never been easy for us we made it.. ..We had a wonderful time till 2 o clock ..We had been enjoying every single seconds with out losing it.. We took a few pictures we're chocolates cakes ice cream everything...But at the end we become sad while leaving... Then somehow we both told bye ...Really difficult to say bye after spending hours together..Then right here is the twist missed my bus then i booked a bus again...

Then once more the whole thing become normal, we started yearning once morewe started missing again..We actually planned to meet 6 months once..Soo we have been anticipating the following meet.

Nothing interesting after that meet we have been simply looking forward to the next meet.. We have been counting dates and i used to be saving money ..She is my best friend till now..I share everything with her and she shares everything with me ..For me she is my best friend ..We used to gossip things.. Really blessed to get a girlfriend like her..

SECOND MEET (4-8-2021)

Months passed,we decided to meet once more as it have been four to five months soo we determined to meet..I dont remember why my mother and father and me went to madurai .. I Booked a bus, August third nighttime from Dindigul ..told my mom that i will be going to my college friend house..He was in Dindigul, so i went to Dindigul and took my bus...Me and ishu were talking for the whole time while i was traveling..We both were soo excited, nervous, happy it was mixed emotions...I hate to travel at day time,i become so tired, hungry too..I used to inform everytime while i'm going there i used to be like i am here, there and that i noticed this one that one ..I reached there at 10 o clock.. This time i Book an hotel room...I became soo tired and could not sleep.. That is the first time i'm staying someplace with out my parents..But whenever i go there i'd get new experience..Back to the story.. She was in call till i sleep.. next day morning i awakened at 7 30 something..I became very very excited, blushings..It was soo cold there that's the first time i'm staying in Coimbatore... We texted for sometimes ..Was looking forward to her moms and dads to go away home.. Then she told me to come ,i booked a ola was waiting for it to come..Then the same like last time i got off from ola and walked to her home..

Like last time she was there in 1st ground saying hello and instructed me to move in the house..She got here we hugged..this time we had been now no longer like before, no worried nothing... We began out talking..I Still recall the way it went..It become special without a doubt ..No phrases describe approximately the meet.. We loved properly spent a few treasured time of my life..She fed me curd rice, we captured a video and i still have that one.. What else we had a wonderful time together, happiest day of my life.... While leaving we gave a good hug...Soo returned to normal..Our love tale isn't always like others, we must await nearly four to five months to spend time.. **untill (4-8-2021) HAPPY BIRTHDAY ISWARYA**

TO BE CONTINUED...